DIZZY
IN
YOUR
EYES

DIZZY IN YOUR EYES

POEMS ABOUT LOVE

PAT MORA

Alfred A. Knopf
New York

THIS IS A BORZOI BOOK PUBLISHED BY ALFRED A. KNOPF

Copyright © 2010 by Pat Mora

All rights reserved. Published in the United States by Alfred A. Knopf, an imprint of Random House Children's Books, a division of Random House, Inc., New York.

Knopf, Borzoi Books, and the colophon are registered trademarks of Random House, Inc.

Visit us on the Web! www.randomhouse.com/teens

Educators and librarians, for a variety of teaching tools, visit us at www.randomhouse.com/teachers

Library of Congress Cataloging-in-Publication Data
Mora, Pat.
Dizzy in your eyes : poems about love / by Pat Mora. — 1st ed.
p.   cm.
ISBN 978-0-375-84375-4 (trade) — ISBN 978-0-375-94565-6 (lib. bdg.) —
ISBN 978-0-375-89601-9 (e-book)
1. Love—Juvenile poetry. 2. Love poetry, American. 3. Young adult poetry, American. I. Title.
PS3563.073D59 2010
811'.54—dc22
2009004300

The text of this book is set in 12-point Galena.

Printed in the United States of America
January 2010
10 9 8 7 6 5 4 3 2 1
First Edition

With gratitude, to my editor,
Nancy Hinkel

CONTENTS

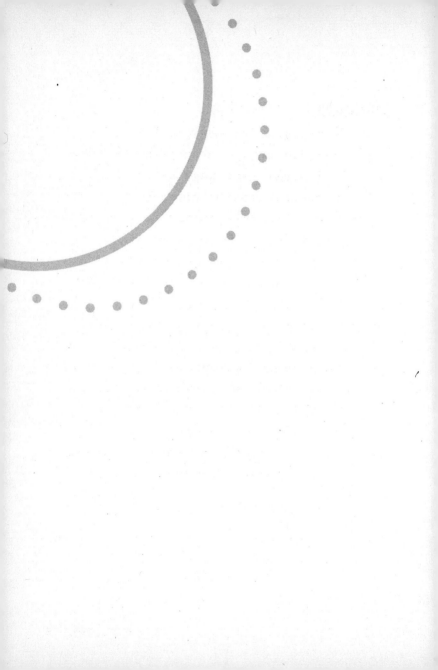

Dear Reader,

I love the intensity of the teen years. Friends, family, causes—peace, justice, the environment—matter in new ways. Our emotions are also turned UP, and some days we look at someone and feel dizzy in their eyes.

I began this collection in free verse, poems written without emphasis on counting syllables or stresses. My editor, Nancy Hinkel, suggested that I also try some poetic forms like sonnets or haiku to show my readers the options and challenges that such forms can pose. Although initially writers of any age might frown at forms, once we begin to play with the possibilities, we're surprised at the interesting results.

The *clerihew* (KLER-uh-hyoo), for example, a form seldom used, was invented by Edmund Clerihew Bentley. A person's name (often a famous person) is the first line, and using the *aabb* rhyme pattern, the poem pokes gentle fun at the subject. Since it's fun to play with a form, I decided to write a clerihew about a very unfamous person: me.

Pat Mora,
una señora, autora, platicadora
so daffy, she thinks words sweet as candy,
so keeps her thesaurus handy.

Good thing I'm bilingual in Spanish since it's hard to find a rhyme in English for *mora,* which literally means "mulberry." Want to try writing a clerihew using your name?

I enjoyed writing these poems for you and hope that you enjoy reading them or using them as duets or for choral reading—or setting them to music. One of the final challenges of a collection is deciding the order for the book. As I reread the poems slowly, I began to think of the book as a piece of music with four movements that we could call a love cycle: from love's initial rush and confusion, to love's challenges, heartaches, and quiet sadness; to external solace that eases the pain, necessary healing; and finally, yes, to falling in love again. An important and sustaining love in our lives is hearing and valuing our own unique, internal song.

Pat Mora

January 2010

Weird

I start to type an e-mail, but
the letters on the screen don't match
the letters I type. I try again,
stare at the screen,
feel I'm in some weird movie
and the machine is possessed,
has learned to read
my mind
and enjoys watching my confusion,
knows I can't tell anyone:
      my computer and I
have a secret.
      They'll think I'm crazy.

No matter what I do,
the keys type your name.

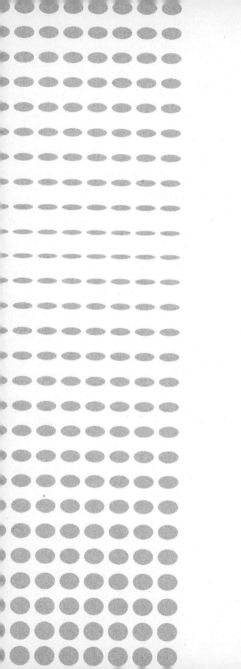

I Can Dance

I can dance,

moving muscles and knees,
shoulders and hips,
smart as you please.

I can dance,

like the guys on TV,
like the dudes on the street,
feeling free and at ease.

I can dance,

the old and the new,
baby, I've got the beat.
Watch my steps. It's a breeze—

in my room alone

with the door closed.

Tercet (TUR-sut, from the Italian, meaning "third"): A three-line stanza or poem, often rhymed. I recast this poem and "Fortune Cookie" (on page 23) in tercets because the number three is emphasized in the poems.

Revenge x 3

I slipped a note to three—
the same note—Romeo me,
experienced at poetry.

All three were sweetly pretty.
Each read my words, smiled slyly.
I felt clever and happy.

My life would be a movie—
calls to make, hands to hold lightly,
poems to write nightly.

But one day, three came frowning toward me,
no hint of beauty. Running, I yelled loudly,
"Your frowns will make you ugly!"

Each crowned me—not that lightly.
"Rat!" they shouted, pounding fiercely,
shouted-pounded, "Triple-header!" furiously.

Doubts

What if guys think I can't kiss because I can think?

    What if I ask her out and she laughs?

Why are all the guys I know so short?

    Why do girls like those handsome fakes

    with fast cars and fat wallets?

Can I eat less and less until I'm transparent and shine?

    Why do their eyes squint when we speak Russian?

Do boys really imagine all of us without clothes?

    What if no one wants to touch me because I'm too fat?

Why do they start whispering about me when I walk by?

    When I dance, why do my feet get stuck, as if music

    is a foreign language?

Does anyone care about the real me?

    Does my breath smell like a fish tank?

Why don't they like him just because he's Muslim?

    What if the way I kiss is dull, like oatmeal?

Why do adults say, "What do you know about love?"

    Why is my dog the only one who really understands me?

How does it feel to be married?

    Why do my parents kiss in public?

If I sing better than she does, why don't I get up there and sing?
  Why do teachers all think I'm dumb as a garbage can?
What will it feel like living far away in a dorm
  with strangers?

              What if, when I leave,
              I crumple
                  by myself?

Mirrors

Grandma makes me mad.
   "You're beautiful. *Tan linda*,"
when I'm studying my face,
boring as old bread,
my wide waist,
   "*Tan linda*,"
my hard-to-hide hips,
my too-flat chest,
my eyes that won't open wide
and round like my sister's,
that hypnotize guys.
   "*Tan linda*."

What does Grandma see?

List poem: A poetic form that catalogs items.

To-do List

1. On Friday, I'll shove all my books into my locker.
   At the click of the lock, I'll smile.
2. I'll ride the bus, smiling at all the people
   who drive me crazy, and drive them a bit crazy too.
3. At home, I'll crank up the music until the walls vibrate
   and make myself a giant sandwich, three-cheese—
   cheddar, Swiss, and pepper Jack—and mustard, mayo,
   lettuce, more cheddar, pickles. I'll fill the biggest bowl
   in the house with chips.
4. If anyone speaks to me, I'll signal that I can't hear,
   while I eat all the chips by myself, smiling.
5. At night, I'll laugh with my friends as we eat our big-
   as-the-table pizza—black olive, sausage, pepperoni, cheese.
6. Saturday, I'll sleep as late as I want. If anyone frowns,
   I will point to my To-do List.
7. A man of leisure, I'll take a walk and nod at everyone
   I see, since my books are safe in my locker. I will also nod
   at any dogs I meet.

8. When my friends come over, I'll sit at my drums and bang
   rhythms that will stop freeway traffic throughout
   the city. Without needing to talk, our band will play
   original songs that recording labels will covet.

9. I'll open a letter from some anonymous donor who sends
   10 ten-dollar bills.

10. At the mall, cute girls will embarrass us
    with their endless flirting, especially with me.

11. Sunday will be a repeat of Saturday except no letter,
    of course, but Mom will surprise me with stacks
    of my favorite foods: tacos, burgers, fries, chocolate chip
    cookies, 3 gallons of ice cream. My To-do List says
    that I may not share—except with my friends.

12. No. This is not some lame dream. I'm a list maker,
    and I know a sensible list when I see one.

Mariachi Fantasy

This afternoon I saw a shiny cholla,
its spines glistening in the sunset,
and I thought of us.
Small and skinny, the cactus
looked like a mariachi
in tight clothes, big charro hat,
head thrown back,

                           singing
letting all his inside feelings

                                    rip

out into the desert
like I'd like to do.

I wondered if his girlfriend,
a nearby cholla looking shy,
like you,
was listening,
pretending not to,
a smile tickling
the edges of her lips.

Fortune Cookie

"Be original," Dad always says.
So how do I ask Libby out—originally?
Clever but secret.

"Want to help?" my sisters ask.
"We're making fortune cookies."
For once, fortunate to have sisters.

Guarding my secret, I write
my question three times to be safe,
hide the paper slips.

We roll and cut dough.
Three times, secretly, I put my question
in the center of a circle.

I fold the dough,
brush it with water,
dip it into colored sugar.

The next day, I toss one by Libby's sandwich.
She breaks the cookie open, laughs,
"Very clever."

"Very original," I say.
"Call me," she says, her mouth
enjoying the sweet pink glitter I taste too.

Back Then

I'd jump on my bike
some afternoons and pedal
by Cecilia's house,
pedaling faster, faster into the wind,
seeing the ordinary house,
sneaking a look as I sailed by
and feeling excited
that she was inside,

not really hoping she'd look out,
just pedaling by, privately
happy that I was near her,
knowing tomorrow at school, she'd smile
at me, and I'd feel like I'd swallowed
a slice of sun.

Valentine to Papi

I kept looking in the mirror
and touching my grown-up hair.
Remember, Papi, ten years ago?
You smiled when you saw me
wearing a new yellow dress.
I was shining for my cousin's wedding.

Your smile
       lit the room.

Strangers who said they were my aunts,
       uncles, great-aunts,
        kept squeezing me.
I'd smooth and straighten my dress.

When the romantic music started,
Mami looked at you
              and pointed at me.
      You looked down
and took my hands,

mine cold, yours warm.
I put my shiny shoes on yours,
and we danced.

Ten years later, in my heart
we still dance
perfectly, Papi.

First Time

Whizz! You jumped and squeezed my arm,
your eyes squinched,
> tense with fear
when the loud bark sank its teeth
> into your neck
as the pickup whizzed by.

We stood there not speaking,
> grateful
in the autumn wind
that we were safe,
> together.
Maybe the driver thought we were wimps
> as he sped by, laughing, mouth open.
Two teens scared of a bark.

> I didn't move.
Your hand warmed mine
> for the first time.

Hands

My aunt watches me
watch Billy. Sly, I try
not to stare at his hands.
"To him, you're just Roger's little sister.
He can't see you," my aunt whispers.
My aunts always say too much.

Why do they think they know
what I'm feeling? I'm me. Not them.

Billy, my brother's best friend,
the skinny kid
who used to swing me
around, and I'd laugh, feeling free.

I watch Billy's hands
hold the basketball, and I imagine
my hand in his, my eyes
       floating in his brown eyes.

No one has felt like this. Ever.

The Mission

I wake before the alarm
starts its racket.
My English teacher has been saying,
      "Homecoming's in the air.
      Whispers here and there."
I feel the dark
inside and out.
My family's busy dreaming.

In the garage, I lift the flowers
I hid and run softly towards her house.
A dog barks. Stars fade
as the sun's rays light the world.
Roofs appear.

Her house sleeps.
I lay the carnations, roses,
and mums on the hood of her car.
I'm Picasso, admiring my work.
Carefully, I place a few stems on the windshield,

trying to get everything perfect,
irresistible.

"Homecoming's in the air.
Whispers here and there."

Watching the house, I stand back,
arrange and re-arrange the flowers.

Her mother's light goes on,
and I duck behind a bush,
take a last look and run
wondering,

now will she go with me
to the dance?

Grandma's Joke

"Tell me again, Grandma.
Tell me about you and Holland."
Grandma laughs her sweet-as-pansies laugh
that moves to her shoulders,
and they laugh too.
Her eyes begin their dance.

"Start at the beginning.
You and Grandpa in the elevator."
Her laugh keeps slipping out.
        "I wasn't that young,
        but I was dressed hippie-like,
        off to work with my purse and blue scarf.
        A man entered the elevator.
        We were alone.
        We got off on the same floor,
        and the next day, it happened again.
        My heart floated up with the elevator.
        He asked my name.
        I didn't speak much English,

but he started calling. Voilà!
I'd look in the mirror and stare
at my face.
Eventually, he took me to Holland
to meet his family.
They teased us.
Your grandpa's aunt was blind,
but she liked me to visit her.
She'd feel the white
tablecloth, seeing with her fingers.
'No, not this one,' she'd say
to her daughter.
'It's not good enough for her.'

One day, I knelt down on one knee
and asked Grandpa's mother for
his hand. Everyone laughed
at my good joke."

My French grandma!
She proposed to my grandpa.

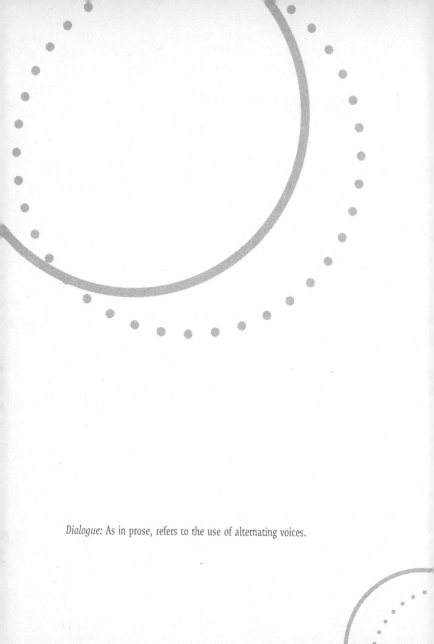

Dialogue: As in prose, refers to the use of alternating voices.

Conversation / Conversación

New here?
Why so sad?

> Sad? *No hablo inglés.*

Oh, but *muy bonita.*

> *Ah, tú hablas español.*

No. Muy poquito. I'm taking Spanish.
You think I sound funny, *¿sí?*

> *No hablo inglés.*
> *Nada.*

Aw, you'll learn. English is easy.

> *¿Eee-zee?*

See. You're learning.
Inglés, muy fácil.

> *Oh, no. Español es fácil.*
> *Inglés es muy difícil.*

Maybe I can teach you
English, and you can teach
me Spanish, *¿sí?*

> *No entiendo.*

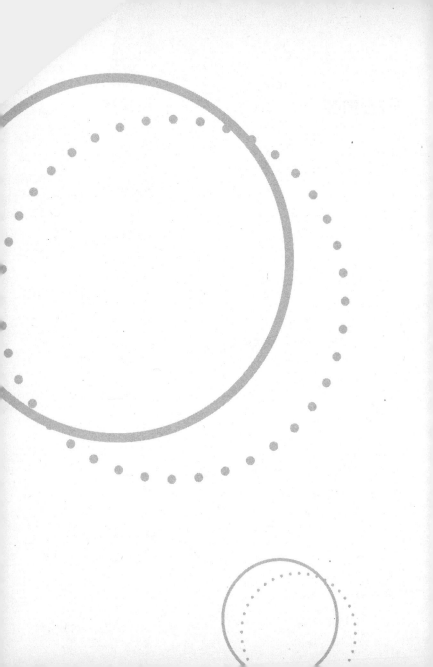

Yo maestro de inglés.
Tú maestra de español.
Oh, so you <u>can</u> laugh.
What's your name, *¿tu nombre?*

                              Me llamo Morena.

Morena bonita.

We look at one another,
wary, but curious,
her eyes, mysterious,
mine, I hope, solicitous.

Slowly, like the sun rising,
she smiles.

Kissing

When my dad saw us kissing
at the bus stop,
            he just drove by.
At home, he said
            nothing.
At dinner, he said
            nothing
so loud the room sounded
like my heart.
"What?" I snapped.

"What's happening?"
Mom asked, reading me
like she did when
I was three,
                  finding
what I couldn't hide.

Dad stared at me,
and I glared back,

our look-alike eyes
locked for days, it seemed—
       maybe people had gone to bed
       and gotten up, gone
       to school—
while Dad and I tangled in silence.
I felt sleepy and worried.
       What if
I dozed and fell off the chair, curled
into a nap right there
by the dining room table
like a child.
       What if
my parents looked at one another,
and Dad gently picked me up
       like in the old days,
carried me,

       but he can't
carry me now.

Dad slapped
      the table.
      "*Basta.* Enough."
We met halfway.
"Don't embarrass yourself,"
he whispered into my hair
when we hugged, and I felt
      the weight
of carrying me.

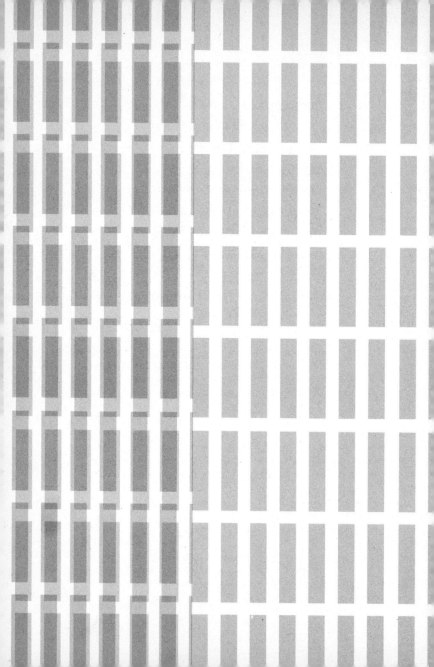

Pressure

The first time
he said "You're beautiful,"
I felt butterflies,
yellow and orange fluttering
on my arms.

When he said "I love you,"
I couldn't feel
my feet.

"Do you love me?"
he asks today, touching
my arm.

He strokes my
hand, and I become
all skin.

My skeleton, the interior
forms that hold me up,
softens into cream.

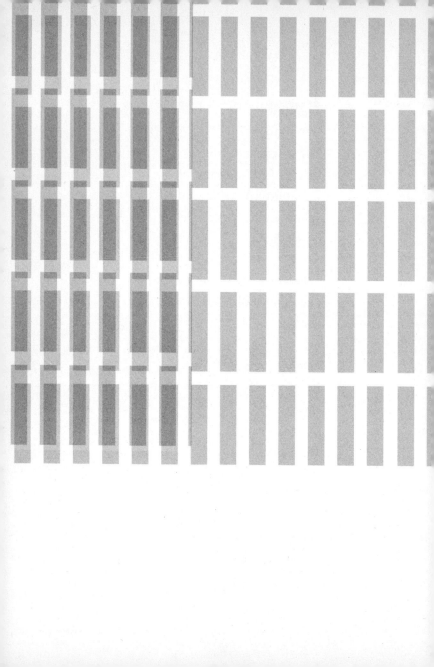

"If you love me,"
he whispers,
barely touching my
lips,
"trust me."

He wants to take me
down to another place,
dark, tangled,
private, just him and me.
       "Trust me—
        if you love me."
But I don't want to go there
yet. What if
I can't find my way back?

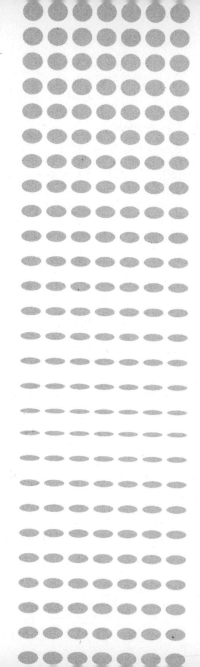

On the Edge

We lived on the edge at high school, circled way out
to avoid their bruises, protecting ourselves from
their stares and snarls at our hair, clothes, tattoos.
To them we were freaks. Know what I mean?

We had our own music, our way of joking,
rushing off on trips so fast we'd forget our wallets,
spending afternoons working on our old cars, laughing
and shouting when the engine would finally catch, and
        we'd sail down the street
honking at people who shot us their frowns.
To them we were freaks. Know what I mean?

When Mike died, our music did too.
We hooked arms by the casket,
wearing the concert T-shirts
Mike had made us buy.
We each said, "He was my best friend."
We talked about how Mike made us laugh,
how we never planned anything,
but stuff always worked out.

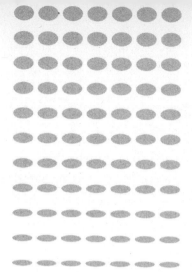

Kids and teachers looked at us up there,
still thinking: what freaks.
Know what I mean?

We each had to speak,
but I wanted just to be silent,
for ten years maybe.

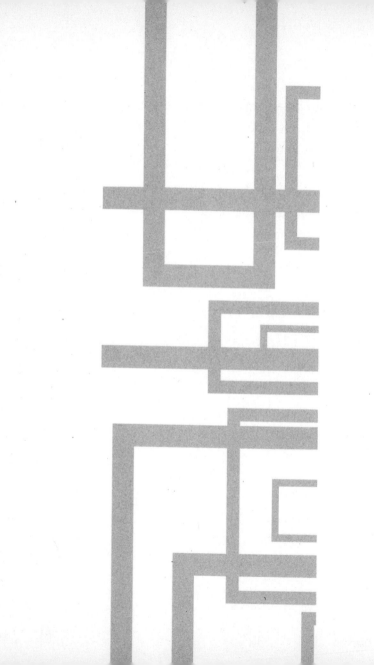

On Guard

I know how
to build fences.
I've built my borders
for years.
Routinely, I repair
attempted entries
into
        my space.
Everyone is suspect,
gray-haired women,
a child's hand
reaching in,
people disguised
as rocks,
all possible invasions.
Don't be deceived:
I savor
my isolation,
my dark interior.
Silence, please.

Your opinions
are unwelcome.
Your jabber,
your many tongues
bore me
but will never bore
into my well-guarded
space. All the un-me
is alien. I take pride
in being on guard.
I'm willing to share
my strategies—
threats, barks,
explosions—
for remaining untouched
          —in here—
by the world's
garbage.

The Silence

We met in kindergarten
and used to laugh often when we turned the pages
of our photo albums, our changing selves.

"So, like, is he your boyfriend?"
My sister's old question. "Boy" an insult,
but not "boyfriend."

He and I always talked,
conversations that lasted for years,
but we never talked about the prom.

Now prom talk everywhere.
I practiced sounding casual. Trying to laugh,
I finally said, "Want to go to the prom with me?"

And then I heard it,

                              the silence

               unraveling years
of jokes, fears, secrets.

He looked like his mouth had blisters
when he said, "I—I—uh, invited someone else."

I didn't cry. I didn't scream.
I didn't
                    "Breathe!" he said roughly.

I turned
and told my reliable legs
to keep moving.

Blank verse: An unrhymed form written in iambic pentameter (iambs are pairs of syllables, the first unstressed, the second stressed; *penta* = five). Each line has ten syllables (five iambs) and can sound conversational. Sometimes, a writer varies the pattern for emphasis as I did in the last line.

Please

I wonder what you do behind hard bars.
I know the "you" the judge will never see.
The family says one day I'll visit you,
but I'm afraid my tears will make you sad.
Inside myself, I hear such scary sounds.
Someone is gasping softly in my skin.

I think of our last dance. I didn't know
I wouldn't dance with you for many years.
They say I have to let myself be mad
that you were selfish and abandoned us,
but what I feel is cold and dark, a pit
I've fallen into where there's not much air.

I tell myself that one day you'll come home.
I'll bake a cake so high your jaw will drop.
You'll smile at me, and we won't need to speak.
I pray for you at night. Do you pray too?
And do you have a night-light where you sleep?
I dream our prayers can meet high in the stars.

I'll write you soon and try to cheer you up.
I hope you have some friends, and food tastes good,
and hope the guards allow you walks outside.
Pretend I'm there. We're walking hand in hand.
Don't let your anger loose at anyone.
Please. Smile. Sing our songs. Let your good shine through.

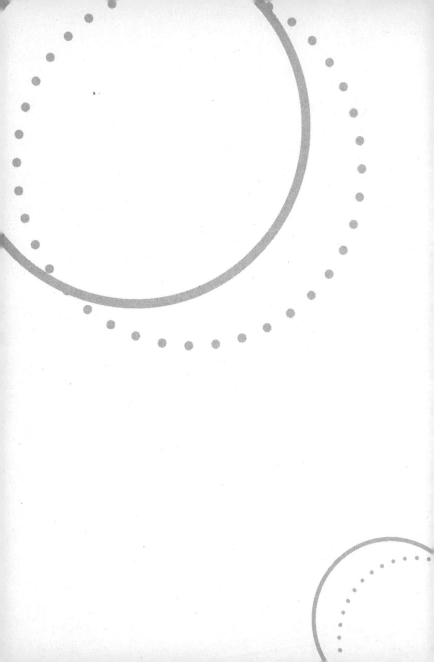

Spanish

My mom worried that I was sick
or changing. *"¿Porqué estás tan quieta?"*
I hurt too much to tell her. I was shrinking
in that school. I couldn't speak
                    English.
All my intelligence and feelings trapped inside,
en español. Quiet. I was the newest
so knew no words. All day I listened and looked
down, hoping no one would ask me a question.
I hid so deep inside, I'd lose myself for days,
forget the sound of my own voice.
At home, I was silent more and more, my mouth
too sad to speak.

When I'd hear *español,* oh!
It surrounded me like a comfort,
una frazada, the syllables soothing
me, slowly thawing my wounded self,
the stranger inside.

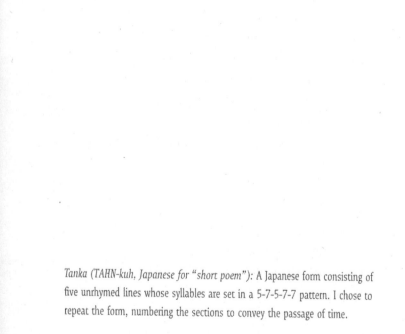

Tanka (TAHN-kuh, Japanese for "short poem"): A Japanese form consisting of five unrhymed lines whose syllables are set in a 5-7-5-7-7 pattern. I chose to repeat the form, numbering the sections to convey the passage of time.

Broken Home?

I

Long, sad, first weekend,
my strange room: a cold, white box.
My brother pouts, cries.
Another first: Dad cooking.
Is our home really broken?

II

Two houses, one home.
Birthdays pull us together.
Singing heals our hurts.
Us four, always family,
a home we make for ourselves.

Letter poem: A poem written in the form of a letter.

Dear _____,

I write what I can't say out loud.
I'm trying not to think about you, but
      I can't resist.
My mind drifts to your slow smile,
      how it moves
from your lips to your eyes—
or is it the reverse? How it lifts me
from my ordinary self.

Do you ever want to hold my hand?

When we're talking, and others join us,
when you laugh with them, I feel tangled
up inside, angry. I struggle not to be rude.
I want to be alone with you.
      I love our aloneness.

When I listen to music, I imagine
slow dancing with you, and you whisper
into my hair, "You are my one true love,"

and I smile
    and know
why people write music and paint
      and dance, lifted as if they can fly,
because this ache
    crashing inside
needs to be free.
    Sometimes, love
becomes a melody
      others hum for years.

Pantoum (pan-TOOM, from the Malay word pantun): A poetic form, usually rhyming, composed of four-line stanzas (quatrains). Poets have written variations of the repeating pattern in which lines two and four become lines one and three in the following stanza.

Dumped

I can't believe you dumped me.
　　　For months, I felt so happy inside.
What a catastrophe!
　　　Now I feel ugly and just want to hide.

All those months, I felt so happy inside.
　　　Was everything you said untrue?
Now I just want to hide
　　　and try to forget I loved you. Still do.

Was everything you said untrue?
　　　"Let's just be friends." I hate the words.
I'm trying to forget I loved you and still do.
　　　I ache at the mean rumors I've heard.

"Let's just be friends." Haunting words.
　　　Me, a lump you dumped, casually.
How I ache at the rumors I've heard.
　　　My heart broke, my private catastrophe.

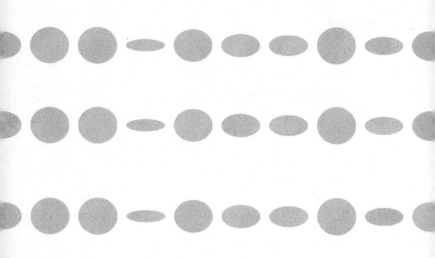

Sestina (seh-STEE-nuh, from the Italian, meaning "sixth"): A fixed poetic form
of thirty-six lines that is like a verbal dance. The author chooses six words that
will be the final words of six unrhymed lines in six stanzas. The pattern for
the repetition is established in stanza one and follows the end-word pattern of
6, 1, 5, 2, 4, 3. Often three additional concluding lines contain all six words.

Questions

When she asked me out for coffee,
I knew she was different.
Her words were funny but lonely.
Her eyes nervously asked questions.
I was looking into a murky well,
but I couldn't turn away.

Sometimes I wish I could take her away.
We could walk a beach sipping coffee,
and she'd laugh and feel really well
and not start crying. She'd be different.
No one would ask me questions
about being with someone so weird, lonely.

"Save me," she whispers. It makes me lonely.
My life before that first day seems far away.
Her cutting habit scares me. I ask questions
so maybe she can say what hurts. I offer coffee
with lots of sugar and milk, something different.
She dries her smudged eyes, sighs, "Oh, well."

I wish we could hold hands by a rock well
and fling in her thorny wounds, fears, loneliness.
Maybe things with her will never be different.
Maybe I need to pack up and run far away,
but then tomorrow, alone, she'd drink bitter coffee
again, and I'd be asking myself what-if questions.

My counselor asks me confusing questions
about whether I can cure her, make her well,
and what if I hadn't gone out for that first coffee,
can I really save anyone but me. "But she's so lonely,"
I say, "and I love her and can't just turn away."
I even pray that she'll wake up smiling, different.

My family says, "Think of college, a new different
life, a clean start." Maybe a roommate will question
my politics, sign us up for a trip to mountains far away.
Can, should I, forget her, and focus just on me? Well,
I'd miss her too, digging into my skin, lonely
for what I provide, warmth and not just in the coffee.

People say I don't look well. I stopped coffee,
but the broken questions just replay, won't go away.
I want to be different even if I'm lonely.

Old Love

When my aunt died,
my uncle raised his hands
like a prophet in the Bible.
"I've lost my girl," he said,
"I've lost my girl," over and over,
shaking his head.

I didn't know what to say,
where to look,
my quiet uncle raising his voice
to silence.

My aunt was eighty-seven.
"Listen," my uncle said, sighing
like a tree alone at night,
"women know.
Every midnight on New Year's Eve,
when others sang
and laughed and hugged,
your aunt looked at me,

tears in her eyes.
Sixty years.
She knew.
One day, we'd kiss good-bye."

Villanelle (vih-luh-NEL, plural form of villanella, *an Italian country song):* This challenging but rewarding form consists of a pattern of nineteen lines—five tercets and a concluding quatrain. Two rhyming refrains braid through the poem, and a second rhyme occurs within every stanza. Many poets have enjoyed varying this pattern.

Our Private Rhyme

I wish we could go back in time.
I thought you'd live forever.
I feel I'm only half our rhyme.

You left and somehow I must climb
back to live without your laughter.
Can't we please go back in time?

I try to smile, pretend and mime
I'm fine, survived disaster
but know I'm only half our rhyme

Will any spring or summertime
shine without your teasing whisper?
I wish we could go back in time.

I hope that you'll forgive my whines.
I'm trying to be braver.
So lonely being half our rhyme.

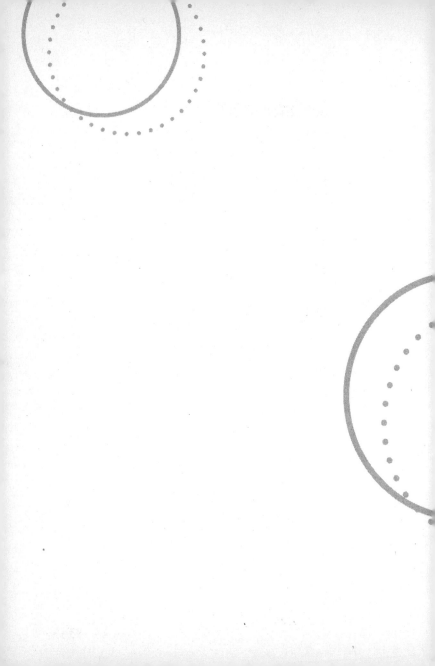

I feel you near. We're intertwined.
Your spirit makes me stronger.
I know we can't go back in time.
I'll strive to be our private rhyme.

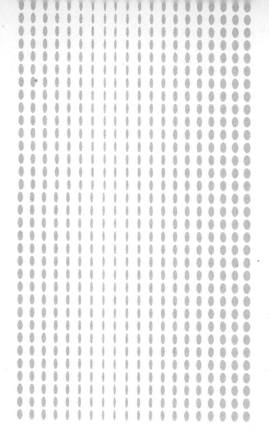

Sonnet (from the Italian, meaning "little song"): A fourteen-line poem, usually rhyming and usually in iambic pentameter (see page 70). Poets can play with any of these elements. Because sonnets are elegant poems, I purposely chose this form to describe a family that might not be viewed as elegant. I wanted to suggest that all kinds of people are good topics for all kinds of poems.

The Squeeze

Sundays we squeeze into our low, old car.
We drive to town, excited at the ride.
We cruise by fancy homes—mansions they are—
remind us we live on the other side.
"New people," my mom calls the fancy folks.
"New clothes, new boots, new hats, new hair." We laugh.
"I bet their 'tooths' are shiny new," Sis jokes.
Dad scoffs, "Feed their dogs steaks, our better half."
"Umm, steaks," sighs Grandma, squeezing in a booth.
We order ice cream, payday yesterday.
"Steaks for their dogs," sings Grandma, sighing, soothes
the baby on her lap in her sweet way.
He licks like we did, ice cream from her cone.
She smiles, Grandma and her big *corazón*.

Safety

After the school play, you hugged me
and part of me wanted to stay inside your hugs
the way I used to, resting all safe in the arms
that held me in the beginning, knew me
before I did,
                but
I pulled away and ran to talk and laugh
with my friends. I watched you
watching me move away.
What would people say
if I stayed inside your arms, and
anyway, what if I got stuck
in the warmth and never left?

With Feeling

"Where's the feeling?"
My piano teacher growls,
"Play! Play with feeling!"
        He pinches me, his voice impatient.

My English teacher says, "Write!
Write with feeling!"
She tells us to avoid flat words,
        dull as the bottom of a bucket.

Feeling? I am all feeling.
Don't they see it shimmering
on my skin, plain for all to see?
        I burn with feeling.

I struggle to contain
tears, giggles, fears, hates, anger,
and love, so much love, all have me spinning
        in my purple-green-red-black-yellow private vortex.

Far Away

My grandmother is far away.
I won't hear her say again,
"Remember how we used to play,
and how I always let you win?"
and pat my hand.

My mother is there now, far away,
whispering in the other language
she lives in. She prays.
She feeds my grandmother with a tiny spoon
food soft as bits of sugared air.

My mother smoothes her mother's hair.
I see them far away,
speaking with their eyes, love spilling

down

their skin, here and there.

Songs

People are songs.
Some stumble along
trying to find the right key.
Some specialize in dirges,
always moaning about their aches
and others' mistakes.
Some chirp-chirp automatically,
like old cuckoo clocks.

"I'm like an old tree, sweetie,
still singing in the wind,"
my grandfather would say to me.
Standing in front of his congregation,
my grandfather's body sang,
listening
to a higher song, harmonizing.
Afterwards, a gentle joke, a wink, a hug,
lifting us all up.

The night before he died, he sang
an old love song to my grandmother.
I bet he held her hand.
I imagine his voice rising and falling
like an old tree, and when he died,
he was singing a hymn, praising
          the Lord.
My grandfather, a holy song.

Cinquain (sing-KANE, from the Latin word quinque, *meaning* "five"): A five-line stanza or poem, often written in five unrhymed lines of 2-4-6-8-2 syllables.

Mundo de agua

Sliding
into blue pool
swirl of my other world,
recurring rhythm: breath, stroke, kick,
wet home.

Stretching
into my breath,
I reach beyond myself,
earth-sounds muffled, water and I
alone.

Racing,
I gasp, we gasp,
then cheer our team on, hoarse
from the hunger, all our practice,
we're one.

Anaphora (uh-NAF-or-uh, from the Greek, meaning "to bring back or repeat"): The use of a repeated word or phrase at the beginning of a series of sentences or verses.

Sisters

It's nice having a sister,
especially if she's older
and quickly outgrows her clothes.

It's nice having a sister,
especially if she's a shopper,
and you laugh together until it hurts.

It's nice having a sister,
especially when you both pick on your brother
and tell your mother, "It's his fault."

It's nice having a sister,
especially when you can join her
and her friends for pizza or a burger.

It's nice having (or finding) a sister,
especially when she smoothes her powder
and new makeup—on you.

It's nice having a sister,
especially when boys come over,
and some of them like you better.

It's nice having a sister,
especially when she whispers
a secret your parents don't know.

It's nice having a sister,
especially as together you grow older,
and share years of private laughter.

My Cross-eyed Cat

Shakespeare said, "Love
is in the eye," and
you, O Cat, are my private
prize, staring eye
to eye, warm fluff,
too old—sorry—
too regal to run,
you saunter
into the sun's irresistible lullaby,
doze worryless,
content, then stretch,
and s t r e t c h in the warm
comfort. Deep in your fur,
you track me
without moving, then,
with the patience of age—
drawn to me
like a moth to a bulb's warm
song—you saunter royally to me,
        burrow,

purr in pure pleasure.
You stare at me with your
crossed eyes, my unique,
loyal beauty.

Three Loves

My aunt saw love
strolling in Tokyo's Palace Park,
my traveling aunt
who brings me chopsticks and stories.

I

A man walked his Pomeranian,
then stretched him on a bench
in the sun. A brush in his palm,
the man slowly began to rub
his small, regal dog
in slow, soft circles, their daily rhythm.
The reddish fur and that man's love gleamed.

II

A woman pushed her mother's wheelchair
near a bench, both women in
baseball caps. The daughter turned her mother
toward the sun to warm her bones.
Then the daughter placed her hand
on the knee of the mother, drifting away.

III

A young mother watched her son and daughter run
inside wide, outdoor, roofless rooms,
leafy confinement.
Then the trio sat on round stools.

"Remember? Like us, they were pretending
they sat on toadstools,"
said my traveling aunt
who brings me chopsticks and stories.

Haiku (hi-KOO, from the Japanese, meaning "starting verse"): A three-line, seventeen-syllable poetic form, rhyme optional. The beats per line are fixed at 5-7-5. Since haiku traditionally contain a seasonal reference, I decided to use the four seasons as the settings for four haiku that chronicle a relationship.

Love Haiku

I

Everything's in love.
Birds, butterflies, and now me,
dizzy in your eyes.

II

Love blooms in hot nights.
Under stars, hand-in-hand strolls.
Kisses like star sparks.

III

Now I walk alone.
Did autumn wind cool our love?
No hugs warm me now.

IV

Snow, advise my heart.
White whisper, "Friends. Books. Patience.
Bright new year's coming."

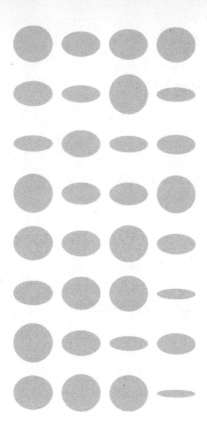

Acrostic (uh-CROSS-tick, from the Greek, meaning "tip of the line"): The initial letters of each opening line spell a word or name, which is also the subject of the poem.

Four-Letter Word

Like breathing, I started when I was born,
        started loving. I didn't know its name,
        but I knew pleasures: eating, warmth.

One day, like a flash of lightning, I linked
        the four letters, the feeling, with the word.
        The word was never the same.

Very soon, I could list loves galore:
        sunshine, Mom's smile, Dad's laugh, our house,
        my bed, jeans, friends; the taste of peppermint,
        music that lifted me soaring off the floor.

Ever since I met you, the word, the same four letters
        became a private place
        your face takes me,
        ours the only keys
        to the invisible door.

Triolet (tree-oh-LAY, from the French, meaning "little trio"): An eight-line fixed form. The first line is repeated in lines four and seven; the second line is repeated in line eight. The rhyming pattern, then, is ABaAabAB.

Lonely Day

I saw your dress sway
with the breeze
at the end of a lonely day.
I saw your dress sway,
drying on a hanger, play,
dance with summer ease.
Softly, I saw your dress sway
and wished I were the breeze.

Blues: This form uses various patterns and combines the African American oral
tradition with the musical blues form. Often about struggle and resistance, a
blues poem can also depict sadness and loneliness.

3 a.m. Blues

It's late—or early. 3 a.m.,
        but six notes keep repeatin'.
Early or late, 3 a.m.,
        those six notes still repeatin'.
I hear your song beginnin',
        slip-slidin' to have you grinnin'.

Your eyes make me want to shine
        so you'll see me.
Your eyes make me want to shine
        so you'll see only me.
Your lips always look a little lonely,
        so I'll sing this song for you only.

Six notes keepin' me awake became
        sway of your walk, whisper of your curves.
Six notes keepin' me awake became
        your walk's sway, whis-whisper of your curves.
And what a shame.
            You don't even know my name.

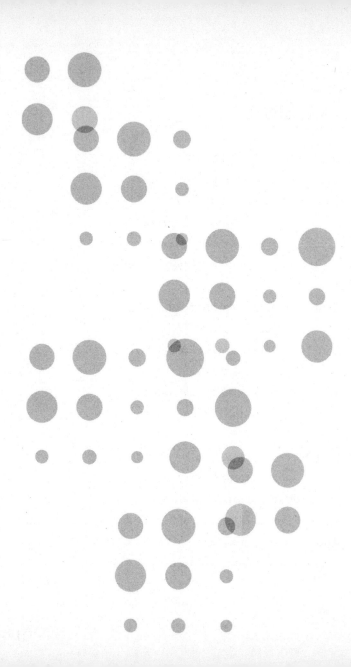

Secrets

I am all secrets now.

I know when you walk into a room.
I don't need to see or hear you
behind me,
      but I know you're there
and wish you'd touch
my shoulder when you walk by.

How can you do that,
without a sound,
      send electricity,
a current
through a room full of people?

When did this crazy secret life start?
People see me but don't see
I've changed.
The me people see isn't the tangled
me inside,

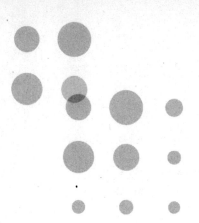

trying not to think
about you,
your laugh
splashing like a waterfall
on a hot summer day.

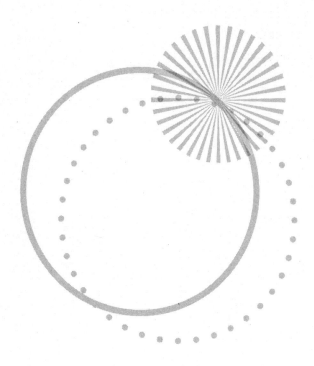

Couplet (CUP-lut): A rhyming two-line stanza or poem.

Opposites

He likes pickles, sour. Me? I like mine sweet.
He likes chocolate ice cream. Vanilla's what I eat.

Big dogs for him, lazy cats for me.
I like to read; he likes TV.

I like to dance; he likes to surf.
He likes to cook, kitchen's not *my* turf.

I like to dress up; he likes to dress down.
I'm kinda nerdy; he's more the class clown.

He likes scary movies I don't want to see.
I'd rather be at a slumber party.

He's very neat; some say I'm messy.
He thinks he's punctual. I sure don't agree.

Loaded burgers for him; I'm a healthy gourmet.
Some predictable stereotypes, from cars to ballet.

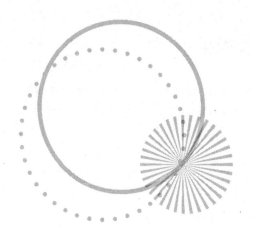

"But together we're great," he'll often repeat.
My funny guy is remarkably sweet.

I confess I'm amazed to be so spellbound
on our wacky opposites merry-go-round.

Lyric (LIR-ick, from the word lyre, a small harplike instrument of ancient Greece that was often played to accompany sung poetry): A form that expresses strong personal feelings.

You're Beautiful

Like the green romance of a bud
and lily's pink, gentle sway.
You: more beautiful than yesterday.

Wildflower's blue surprise.
Daisy's white, sunny play.
You're more beautiful than yesterday.

Orchid's purple mystery.
Mum's bronze *olé*.
You: more beautiful than yesterday.

Rose's orange perfume,
even tulip's yellow secrets say:
you're more beautiful than yesterday.

Poppy's red, teasing lips,
but *your* beauty will never fade.

You.
More lovely than yesterday.

You.
My dazzling bouquet.

Summer Love

Sometimes, we don't even hold hands.
We just stroll and talk about
                                    everything—
the teacher who embarrassed him
last spring, and he turned so red
everyone called him Tomato for a day,

the way my dad frowns
when my friend comes to the door,

my new shoes he likes
because they remind him of green apples.

We watch other couples
and feel happy that now we belong
to the world of twos,

laughing at dogs chasing their tails,
and kids licking their dribbling
ice cream cones,

and we buy two and share our different tastes,
the cool wonder of peach and pistachio,

and discuss whether I should be a dancer
                              or a doctor,

whether we should go to the same college,
and how we could study for hours
and then go out for pizza,
half cheese and half pepperoni.

We talk about going to a movie now,
and I think about his shoulder
next to mine and touching
his hand when we share popcorn,
holding hands when we stroll home,
almost floating in the warm night, and look up
          together
at the dreamy moon.

Mysterious

My paper shines
white, like snow,
but the paper looks empty.
I could decorate it
with tiny spiders
or stars or sketches of me
looking at a blank page,
but the clock ticks, and
somehow I must write.

I like the sight
of untouched snow.
Gentle, slow, silent,
it drifts and swirls,
layers itself, and I see
a new world of mysterious,
inviting shapes. I walk in its white
whispers, *susurrus*.

I drift
back to this paper that feels

hard on the desk, and I begin
        to listen—
to the story I tell myself.

The paper is a white, patient place,
my private space
for remembering,
        saving: spring sun on my face,
venting and inventing,
        arguing with my mother,
wondering: who am I,
        wandering through cobwebs of old dreams,
crying, sighing at people who don't see me,
        hoping to write music so blue
            listeners forget to breathe,
playing the sounds, jamming with myself,

changing
        into the me I can't quite see.

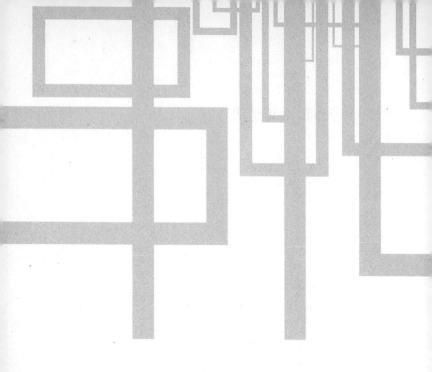

Ode (OHD, from the Greek word meaning "song"): A praise form originally intended to be sung. The Chilean poet Pablo Neruda created short-lined, nonrhyming odes that sang the wonders of ordinary objects such as a bee and salt.

Ode to Teachers

I remember
the first day,
how I looked down,
hoping you wouldn't see
me,
and when I glanced up,
I saw your smile
shining like a soft light
from deep inside you.

"I'm listening," you encouraged us.
"Come on!
Join our conversation,
let us hear your neon certainties,
thorny doubts, tangled angers,"
but for weeks I hid inside.

I read and reread your notes
praising
my writing,

and you whispered,
"We need you
and your stories
and questions
that like a fresh path
will take us to new vistas."

Slowly, your faith grew
into my courage
and for you—
instead of handing you
a note or apple or flowers—
I raised my hand.

I carry your smile
and faith inside like I carry
my dog's face,
my sister's laugh,
creamy melodies,
the softness of sunrise,
steady blessings of stars,
autumn smell of gingerbread,
the security of a sweater on a chilly day.

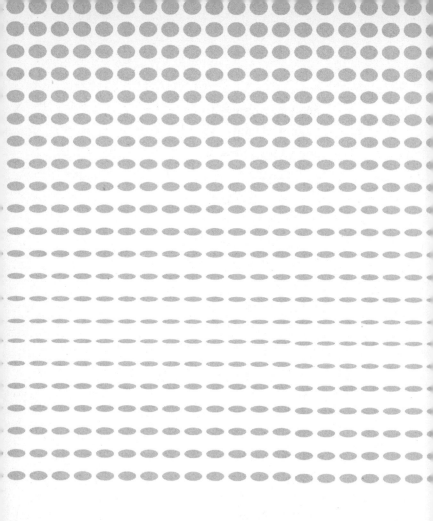

Oda (OH-dah, palabra de origen griego que significa "canción"): Una forma de poesía que elogia. El poeta chileno Pablo Neruda creó una serie de odas compuestas de líneas cortas, sin rima, que celebran los aspectos maravillosos de objetos comunes como la abeja y la sal.

Oda a las maestras

Me acuerdo
del primer día,
como bajé los ojos
con la esperanza
de que no me viera,
y cuando los alcé,
vi su sonrisa
brillando como una luz suave
desde su interior.

"Los estoy escuchando", nos animaba.
"¡Ándenle!
Participen en nuestra conversación.
Déjenos oír sus certezas como luces de neón,
sus dudas espinosas, sus enojos embrollados",
pero durante semanas me escondí en mí misma.

Leí y releí sus notitas
elogiando
lo que escribía,
y usted susurraba:

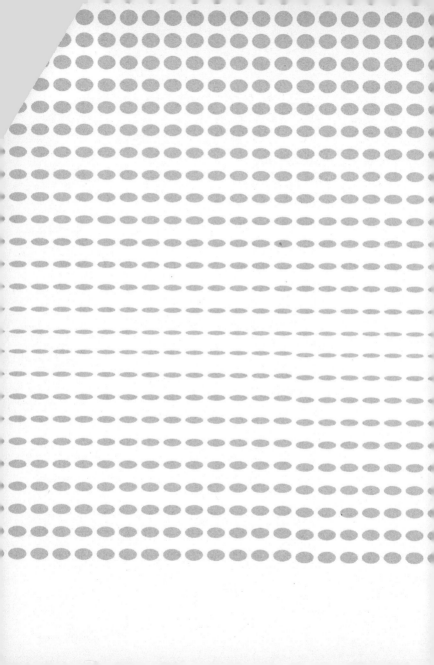

"Te necesitamos.
Necesitamos tus cuentos
y tus preguntas
que, como un fresco sendero,
nos llevarán a vistas nuevas".

Poco a poquito su fe
me dio valor
y para usted—
en lugar de ofrecerle
una nota o una manzana o unas flores—
alcé la mano.

Llevo su sonrisa
y su fe conmigo como llevo
la carita de mi perro,
la risa de mi hermana,
las melodías románticas,
la ternura del amanecer,
las bendiciones constantes de las estrellas,
el aroma otoñal del pan de jengibre,
la seguridad de un suéter en un día frío.

Song: A poetic form designed to be set to music.

My Song

So many memories,
and I'm still young.
So many dreams,
my song's just begun.

Sometimes I hear
my private melody grow,
then the sound vanishes,
but returns, I now know.

I've heard my heart break;
wounded, I've felt alone,
but slowly I learned
to thrive on my own.

I want to keep learning,
to deepen my song;
in whatever I work,
may my best self grow strong.

It's still the morning,
the green spring of my life.
I'm starting my journey,
family and friends at my side,
my song inside,
and love as my guide.

My family wonders
where I will go.
I wonder too.

I long to discover
how to protect the earth, our home,
hear world sisters and brothers,
who feel so alone.

Heart and hands open
to those close and those far,
a great family circle
with peace our lodestar.

No child should be hungry.
All children should read,
be healthy and safe,
feel hope, learn to lead.

It's still the morning,
the spring of my life.
I'm starting my journey,
family and friends at my side,
      my song inside,
and love as my guide.

I'll take wrong turns
and again lose my way.
I'll search for wise answers,
listen, study, and pray.

So many memories,
and I'm still young.
So many dreams;
my own song has begun.

I'll resist judging others
by their accents or skin,
confront my life challenges,
improve myself within.

Heeding my song—
for life's not easy or fair—
I'll persist, be a light,
resist the snare of despair.

Mysteriously,
I've grown to feel strong.
I'm preparing to lead.
I'm composing my song.

It's still the morning,
the spring of my life.
I'm starting my journey,
family and friends at my side,
        my song inside,
and love as my guide.

Acknowledgments

Thanks to Texas librarian Pat Strawn, who proposed this book idea; to my friend, the poet and professor John Drury, for his enthusiasm and for suggestions that always improve my work; and to Pat Smith and the Texas Library Association for their support through the years. Thanks, too, to senior designer Melissa Nelson and assistant editor Allison Wortche.

About the Author

Pat Mora is the award-winning author of many books. Her books for adults include six acclaimed poetry collections, an essay collection, and a family memoir, *House of Houses*. Pat received a poetry fellowship from the National Endowment for the Arts and subsequently served as a fellowship judge. She also was awarded a Kellogg National Leadership Fellowship and has received two honorary doctorates.

Two of Pat's picture books were illustrated by Raul Colón: *Doña Flor: A Tall Tale About a Giant Woman with a Great Big Heart,* an ALA Notable Book that garnered a Pura Belpré Narrative Honor citation and the Golden Kite Award; and *Tomás and the Library Lady,* winner of the Tomás Rivera Mexican American Children's Book Award. Pat, a literacy advocate, is the founder of the family literacy initiative El día de los niños/El día de los libros, Children's Day/Book Day. A former consultant, museum director, university administrator, and teacher, Pat, the mother of three adult children, is a popular speaker throughout the United States. She is a native of El Paso, Texas, and lives in Santa Fe, New Mexico. To learn more about Pat and her literacy initiatives, please visit www.patmora.com.